AMERICAN INDIAN GAMES

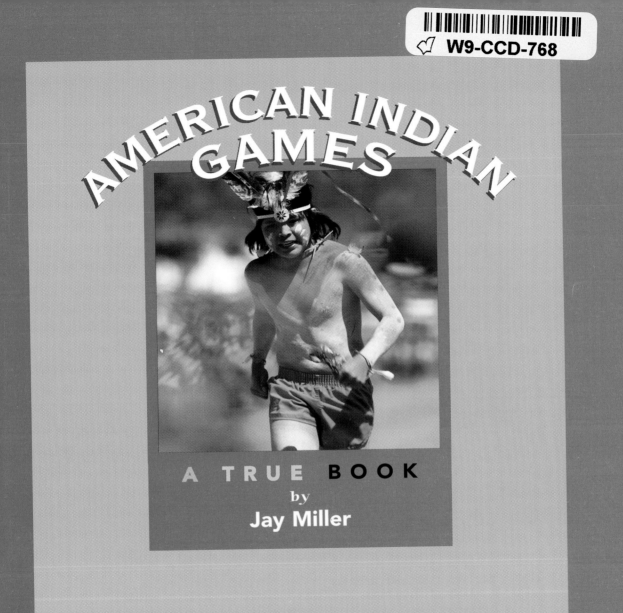

A TRUE BOOK

by

Jay Miller

Children's Press®
A Division of Grolier Publishing
New York London Hong Kong Sydney
Danbury, Connecticut

For help in reading and writing these books, Jay Miller thanks Zachary, Vi, and Rebecca.

Reading Consultant
Linda Cornwell
Learning Resource Consultant
Indiana Department of
Education

Choctaw lacrosse players stretch for the ball.

Library of Congress Cataloging-in-Publication Data

Miller, Jay, 1947-
    American Indian games / by Jay Miller.
      p.   cm. — (A true book)
    Includes bibliographical references and index.
    Summary: Briefly describes some of the toys and games used by
various North American Indian cultures to amuse their children and teach
lessons about life.
    ISBN 0-561-20136-0 (lib. bdg.)   ISBN 0-516-26092-8 (pbk.)
    1. Indians of North America—Games—Juvenile literature. 2. Indians
of North America—Sports—Juvenile literature. [1. Indians of North
America—Games. 2. Indians of North America—Social Life and
Customs.] I. Title. II. Series.
E98.G2M55 1996
394'.3'08997—dc20   96-13477
                                            CIP
                                            AC

Contents

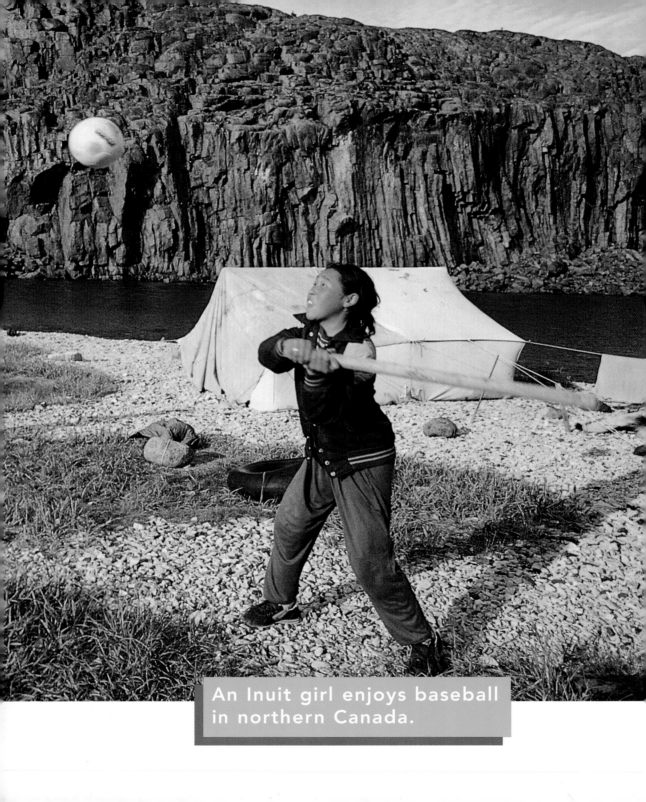

An Inuit girl enjoys baseball in northern Canada.

Why Play Games?

All over the world, people play games for many reasons. Most people play games because they are fun. But games also can build strong bodies and teach people about sharing and taking turns.

When American Indians play, they remember that games must be played in the right way. Tsimshians, in British Columbia, Canada, tell a story about what happens to noisy children.

Once there was a town where children played games loudly every day. Heaven got angry and sent a feather to float above the town.

The children tried to grab the feather. They stood on each other's shoulders until the chief's son got hold of it and could not let go. Every-one became attached to him

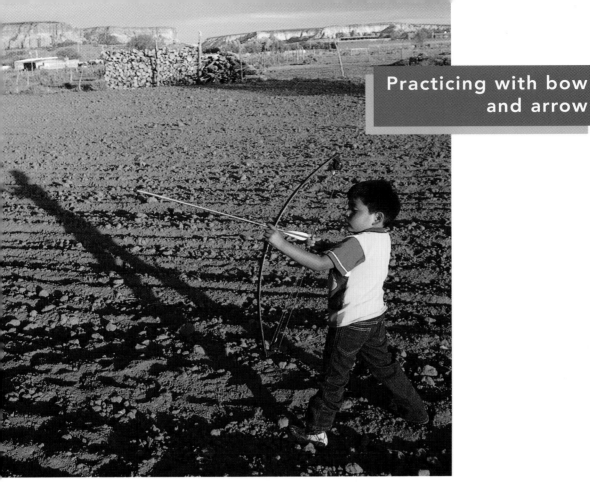

and slowly rose into the air. They were never seen again.

Most of all, games helped American Indians to survive. Many Indians hunted animals with bows and arrows. So

Hopi boys shoot arrows through a hoop, almost 90 years ago.

boys all over the Americas practiced using toy bows and arrows to hit a target or a rolling hoop. That took a good eye and careful aim.

Arctic Ocean

Inuit

Inuit

Inuit

Copper
Eskimos

Northwest

Tsimshian

Pacific Ocean

Makah

Plains

Lakota Cheyenne

Oglala

Sauk Iroquois

Potawatomi Mohawk

Delaware

Southwest

Hopi Zuni

Southeast

Choctaw

Atlantic Ocean

ORTH AMERICAN
TRIBES

Gulf of Mexico

Caribbean Sea

Toys

American Indian children played games with many kinds of toys.

Many girls had dolls. On the Plains, dolls were made from corn husks, mud, or deerskin. Dolls did not have faces. Lakota girls played house with small tipis.

Toys a Lakota child might have used (top); a carefully made doll—with no face (bottom left); Oglala girls play with tipis in the 1890s (bottom right)

"Jabber" toys could
be made in many
different ways.

Boys didn't only play with bows and arrows. The jabber, or cup and pin game, kept eyes and hands working together. It was a pointed stick with a string tied to the back end. Attached to the other end of the string were some objects. Players tried to jab the pointed end at the dangling objects until all of them were speared.

In places such as the North-west, where people traveled by water, children had tiny canoes to learn how to paddle and deal with water flow and dangers.

After it snowed on the Plains, children used sleds made of buffalo ribs tied together. They slid down hills and slopes. Sometimes they ended the trip on frozen streams so they slid far.

A sled made from buffalo ribs

15

Just for Fun

Many games weren't only for children. For fun, everyone learned to make complicated figures using string on their fingers. This game is called cat's cradle, after the name of one of the patterns the string can make. It is played today.

Women were fond of playing with dice, which they

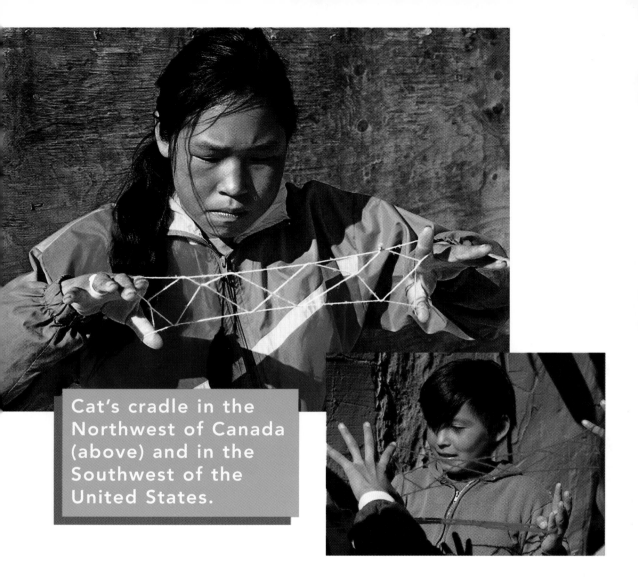

Cat's cradle in the
Northwest of Canada
(above) and in the
Southwest of the
United States.

made from fruit pits, bone,
wood, or beaver teeth. Each
side was painted with different colors, or decorated with

A dice game as it used to be played (above); a Potawatomi bowl and dice (top right); some Cheyenne dice and their carrying bag (bottom right)

dark lines and dots. Each pattern meant a certain number of points. The dice were tossed inside a basket or wooden bowl. If the dice landed with all the same

design up or down, that count-
ed extra.

Men played a guessing game
in which an object was hidden
under one of four moccasins. A
man on the other team had to
guess where a small object,
such as a nut, was hidden.

Under which moccasin
is the nut?

Preparing for Life

Games were also part of growing up. Some tribes had baby-talk words that made everyone laugh, or "tongue twisters" that were hard to say. This practice taught people to be careful about what they said and how they said it.

Everywhere, young women

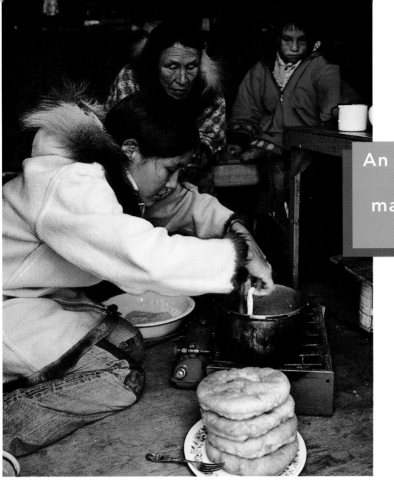

An Inuit teenager learns how to make bannock, a kind of bread.

played house. They did what the women did to take care of their families. They cooked and cleaned. On the Plains, they pretended to butcher buffalo.

21

In the high, dry lands near the Rockies, they gathered and roasted seeds.

Young men learned to wrestle and play at other sports to grow strong and agile. Teams would pretend to be enemies and fight. They learned to dodge in pretend fights with mud balls or snowballs. They practiced ignoring pain to be brave warriors. In these serious games, they learned to go without food and water and to ignore bruises and

Young Mohawks of today train in a survival school (top). Canoe race on the coast of British Columbia (bottom)

cuts. They wanted to be ready for battles with other tribes or Europeans.

In the Northwest, towns had their warriors race war canoes. Each one had a crew of twelve paddlers. This kept them ready for battle or attack.

Young and old men tested their strength by trying to lift and carry heavy rocks. Often these boulders were decorated with paint or designs chipped into the surface.

During the winter, men or boys played snowsnake. They took turns hurling a ten foot long spear along a groove in the snow or on the ice. The one whose spear went farthest won.

Part of a Team

Some American Indian nations farmed, and so they lived together in large villages. They developed team games.

In the Southwest, men played a kind of kick ball. A round stone was kicked for miles across the desert. The first team of runners to kick their ball over the goal line won the game. Hopi men grew a long, down-curved toenail to protect their big toes from the hard ball.

In the East, tribes created a game called lacrosse or stickball, now played all over the world.

Old Iroquois lacrosse sticks are not that different from those used today.

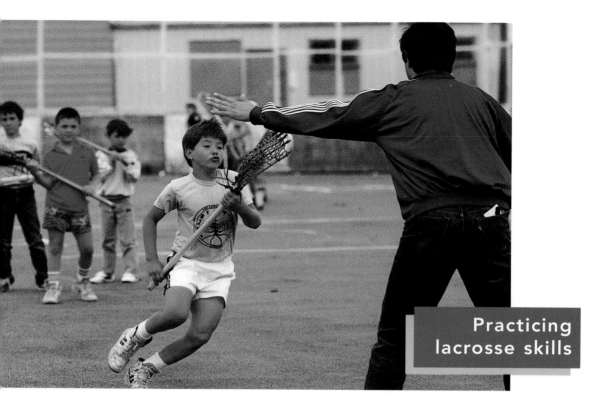

Each lacrosse player has a
racket, a stick with a net on the
top end. Iroquois and most
other players use only one
racket. Tribes of the Southeast,
like the Choctaw, use two
rackets, one in each hand.
Players try to get a three-inch

27

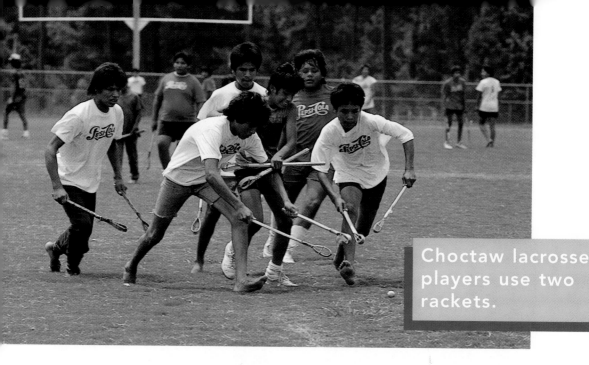

ball made of wood, or of buck-
skin stuffed with hair, into the
net and carry it over the goal
line. Each side can have only a
few members. In big games,
there may be hundreds of men.

According to one legend, the
first lacrosse game was played
by animals against birds. At first,

neither side wanted the bat on their team. But the animals finally let him play. They won, because the bat could run and fly. Since then, Choctaw players ask the bat for help. Some will wear something from a bat for luck.

Choctaw players still dress in special ways for luck. Some will play in bare feet or wear a necklace of horsehair because horses run fast. Sometimes, they ask a holy man to pray for them. They believe that it is good to be brave and strong, but not enough. Players with the strong-est help from the spirits win.

Long ago, women in many tribes played shinny, a game like today's field hockey. Each player used a stick with a curved end to hit a ball made of wood, or stuffed leather, along the ground.

The Makah in the Northwest played shinny with two curved sticks. Each player used one for hitting the ball and the other for carrying it to the goal. They played the game after one of

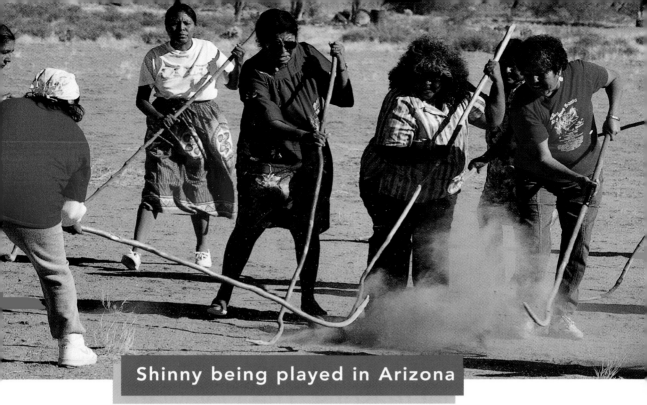

Shinny being played in Arizona

their leaders had harpooned a whale and brought it to the beach. Everyone feasted and then played shinny using a soft whale bone as the ball.

Today, shinny is still a popular game among American Indians.

Special Games

Some games were played for special reasons. The Delaware played a ball game all summer long to help their crops grow.

Men played against women. The men could only kick the ball, made of leather stuffed with deer hair, and the women could only throw it with their hands. It was like the men were playing soccer and the women were playing football. To win, a team had to take the ball through two goal posts at the east or west end of a long field.

The game was held as a prayer to Corn Mother and the crops. During summer play, the crops grew. In the fall, the Delaware stopped playing because the crops were ready to harvest.

Games were sometimes used to settle arguments. Copper Eskimos of the Canadian Arctic held song duels. Instead of coming to blows, people who were angry with each other sang insulting songs about the other person. A crowd listened, and the person with the most clever song won.

When the Hopi town of Oraibi realized in 1906 that its members were not getting

An Inuit gathering — perhaps a song duel is about to happen.

along, they held a tug of war to decide who would leave. The team that got pulled over a line in the sand had to leave the town. The people still live apart.

The Bone Game

When the Spanish came to California, they brought the bone game. Indians learned it. They called this guessing game lahal. They taught it to other tribes. Now everyone in the West plays the bone game.

To play, two teams sit across from each other. A person on one side holds two bone tubes, one plain and the other marked with a black band, in his or her fists.

The other side sings and drums while one of them guesses which hand has the plain bone. The guesser points with his or her finger at one of the fists.

The teams use sticks to keep track of the correct number of guesses. When one team wins all twelve sticks, that side wins the game. Then they start another. Other people bet on the outcome of the games.

New Games

From Europeans, Indians learned to play checkers, dominos, and chess. They carved the figures from wood, bone, stone, and ivory. They made the playing boards of leather, wood, and stone.

Indians also learned how to play card games. They bought

Dominos on Standing Rock Reservation in the 1930s.

the cards from traders or made them from leather or cedar bark. The Delaware made cards from reeds.

Eskimos carved dominos from ivory. They drilled and darkened the dots by hand.

American Indian Games Today

Like modern youngsters everywhere, American Indian youth play baseball, football, basketball, and track and field sports. Many reservation schools have won regional and state titles in these sports.

Two American Indian junior-high football teams in New Mexico (top)
A Zuni Pueblo high-school cross-country team (bottom)

The great Jim Thorpe in a football kicking contest (left)
The Carlisle Indian School football team in the 1890s (above)

The most famous Indian athlete of modern times was Jim Thorpe, a Sauk from Oklahoma. He played football, baseball, and track and field for the Carlisle Indian School in

Pennsylvania. He also won gold medals in the 1912 summer Olympics.

Today, American Indians excel in every modern sport. Yet, they still like to compete in traditional sports such as canoeing, lacrosse, and lahal.

To Find Out More

Here are more places to learn about American Indian games:

 Books

 Organizations

Bierhorst, John, ed. **Lightning Inside You, and Other Native American Riddles.** William Morrow and Company, 1993.

Bierhorst, John, ed. **The Sacred Path: Spells, Prayers, and Power Songs of the American Indians.** William Morrow and Company, 1983.

Blood, Charles L. **American Indian Games and Crafts.** Franklin Watts, 1981.

Crum, Robert. **Eagle Drum: On the Powwow Trail with a Young Grass Dancer.** Four Winds Press, 1994.

American Indian Athletic Hall of Fame
Haskell Indian Junior College
Lawrence, KS 66044

National Museum of the American Indian
Smithsonian Institution
470 L'Enfant Plaza SW
Suite 7103, MRC 934
Washington, DC 20560
Runner@IC.SI.EDU

National Park Service
Office of Public Inquiries
P.O. Box 37127
Washington, DC 20013
(202) 208-4747
http://www.nps.gov

The Southwest Museum
234 Museum Drive
Los Angeles, CA 90065
(213) 221-2164
swmuseum@annex.com

A Guide to the Great Sioux Nation
http://www.state.sd.us/state /executive/tourism/sioux/ sioux.htm

Explore landmarks, legends, art, powwows, and other interesting traditions of the Sioux Nation.

American Indian Resources
http://www.ihs.gov/ 1AmerInd/AI.html

This site contains a complete list of all American Indian tribes, information about them, and links to other sites.

National Museum of the American Indian
http://www.si.edu/organiza/ museums/amerind/

Part of the Smithsonian Institution, this online site is filled with interesting facts and exhibits about Western Hemisphere Indians.

Native American Art Gallery
http://www.info1.com/ NAAG/index.html

Browse the catalog of art and artists and sign up for the gallery's newsletter.

Native Web
http://web.maxwell.syr.edu/ nativeweb/index.html

Discover information about indigenous people all over the world.

Important Words

arrow a stick with feathers on the end and a chipped stone point: shot with a bow, a flexible piece of wood with a strong cord tied to both ends

canoe a small boat made from a hollowed out log or from a wooden frame covered with sheets of bark

culture ideas, actions, and habits that children learn as they grow up in a certain group of people

duel a kind of fight with special rules between two people

moccasin a soft shoe made of leather

spirit an invisible being with special powers

warrior someone trained to fight in battles for his nation

Index

Meet the Author

J ay Miller lives in Seattle, visiting nearby reservations, mountains, streams, and the Pacific Ocean. He enjoys eating salmon and pie, hiking in the mountains, and kayaking along the shore as much as he enjoys being a writer, professor, and lecturer. He has taught in colleges in the United States and Canada. He belongs to the Delaware Wolf clan. His family is delightful and very complex. He has also authored *American Indian Families*, *American Indian Festivals*, and *American Indian Foods* for the True Book series.